Flutter, Kick

Flutter, Kick

poems

Anna V. Q. Ross

2020
Benjamin Saltman
Poetry Award

Red Hen Press | *Pasadena, CA*

Book Layout by Margot Heron

Library of Congress Cataloging-in-Publication Data

Names: Ross, Anna (Anna V. Q.), author.
Title: Flutter, kick : poems / Anna V. Q. Ross.
Description: First edition. | Pasadena, CA : Red Hen Press, [2022]
Identifiers: LCCN 2022007376 | ISBN 9781636280455 (paperback) | ISBN
  9781636280868 (ebook)
Subjects: LCGFT: Poetry.
Classification: LCC PS3568.O841986 F59 2022 | DDC
  811/.54—dc23/eng/20220218
LC record available at https://lccn.loc.gov/2022007376

The National Endowment for the Arts, the Los Angeles County Arts Commission, the Ahmanson Foundation, the Dwight Stuart Youth Fund, the Max Factor Family Foundation, the Pasadena Tournament of Roses Foundation, the Pasadena Arts & Culture Commission and the City of Pasadena Cultural Affairs Division, the City of Los Angeles Department of Cultural Affairs, the Audrey & Sydney Irmas Charitable Foundation, the Meta & George Rosenberg Foundation, the Albert and Elaine Borchard Foundation, the Adams Family Foundation, Amazon Literary Partnership, the Sam Francis Foundation, and the Mara W. Breech Foundation partially support Red Hen Press.

First Edition
Published by Red Hen Press
www.redhen.org

ACKNOWLEDGMENTS

Many thanks to the editors and publishers of the following journals, in which these poems first appeared, at times in earlier versions.

The Baffler: "Almost a Mothering"; *Beloit Poetry Journal*: "The Algorithm Thinks I Need a Girdle," "She threw herself upon the coffin"; *Brooklyn Quarterly*: "Arithmetic," "Self-Portrait as Smaller Moon," "Self-Portrait without Wings"; *Harvard Review Online*: "Back Porch Aubade"; *The Kenyon Review*: "Not if, but when"; *Los Angeles Review*: "Heaven Knows," "Hypothesis"; *Mom Egg Review*: "Heaven Knows," "Wrestling with Gods"; *The Nation*: "After All"; *Pangyrus*: "Causes Unknown"; *Poetry Northwest*: "What Is the Poem"; *Provincetown Arts*: "At Collinsville Bridge"; *Salamander*: "All Hallows," "Self-Portrait as Fox in Daylight," and "Self-Portrait Instead of Engine"; *Southern Humanities Review*: "Explaining Tampons to My Son," "Fugue," "My Son Hands Me the *Family Letter About This Unit*," "One Time," "Self-Portrait with Refrain," "Studies Show"; *The Southern Review*: "Self-Portrait with Washing Machine"; *The Sow's Ear*: "Real Life"; and *Tupelo Quarterly*: "Self-Portrait with Alternate Ending."

"Self-Portrait at Treeline" appears in *More Truly and More Strange: 100 Contemporary Self-Portrait Poems*, edited by Lisa Russ Spaar.

"Self-Portrait with Alternate Ending" appears in *City of Notions: An Anthology of Contemporary Boston Poems*, edited by Danielle Legros Georges.

"One Time" takes its first, second, and fifth lines from the caption to Shelly Julian Bunde's painting *This is Mrs. Lawrence Schlegel from outside of Hettinger, North Dakota*. 2013, acrylic on wood panel.

Thanks to composer Scott Wheeler for his song setting of "One Time," which is included (under the title "She Left for Good One Time") in the recording *Between Us All: New American Art Songs for Voice & Guitar* by The Bowers Fader Duo.

"She threw herself upon the coffin" is for Elizabeth Cardoso and in memory of Jonathan Cardoso.

I'm grateful to the following programs and institutions for their support in the writing of these poems: Massachusetts Cultural Council, the Poetry Program at the Community of Writers, Vermont Studio Center, Virginia Center for the Creative Arts, and Sewanee Writers' Conference. Thanks also to my colleagues and the staff of the Writing, Literature & Publishing Department and the Marlborough Institute for Liberal Arts and Interdisciplinary Studies at Emerson College.

Thanks to all at Red Hen, especially Kate Gale, Tobi Harper, Monica Fernandez, and Rebeccah Sanhueza for their attention, kindness, and hard work on behalf of this book.

Thank you to Jeffrey Harrison for selecting the book and for your empathetic and insightful comments on the manuscript. I'm so very grateful.

Enduring gratitude to my many friends, trusted readers and re-readers, and answerers of late-night emails and emergency phone calls and texts, especially Rose McLarney, Melissa Range, Tess Taylor, Austin Segrest, Claire McQuerry, Angela Sorby, Joan Naviyuk Kane, Cheryl Clark Vermuelen, Carrie Bennett, Jessica Bozek, Amaranth Borsuk, Nadia Colburn, Heather Treseler, Kevin McLellan, January Gill O'Neil, Joel Roston, and Veronica Quilligan, to the Quilligan, Ross, Perkins, and Berg families, and above all to my Andy and our Ita Mae & Charlie.

for my parents

in memoriam,
Ita Margaret Quilligan

Contents

House

I come from there, with lavender
growing small against the bricks.
I come from there, with a little white jug
and a tea towel on the tray.
I come from there, with a worn stair rug
and a wooden banister
leading up two floors, past bedroom doors
to a room at the very top
with a window looking down to a square
of grass and a garden wall
where roses grow with tangled canes
rooting between the cracks.
I come from where, I once was told,
someone attached a lock
on her bedroom door and didn't say why
or who she feared
might open it through all the years
she stayed in the house with lavender
grown small against the bricks
and the roses rooting through the wall
and the tea towel on the tray
and the little white jug and worn stair rug
she descended the day she went away.
I come from there.

Self-Portrait as Girl

You were always looking for balloons.
Or not balloons themselves

but the feeling that they might appear
at any moment.

You looked for roads where there should not
be roads, checking them off

inside yourself. In the absence of dogs,
you were brave about dogs.

You felt you should love horses
but preferred trees—the way they moved

without leaving.
Once, you twisted an apple stem

to learn the initials of the man
you would marry. Once,

you held your breath
long enough to swim the pool's width

fastest of all—each blue-green second
marking the length of you—

then gave your apple prize away.

Anxious Talker

There is a place where words are born
of silence, Rumi says.

Is it a place of anxious talkers,
the sort who can't be in an elevator

without remarking on the weather,
not waiting for a response—

How about those Pats? Or a place
for all of us who knew the answer

in second grade but were afraid
to raise our hands and now can't stop

shouting *Seven! It's seven—I know it too!*
at the teacher who praised the one girl

who spoke, shaming the rest of us.
She was the same girl who pulled

your hair at recess if you wore braids
and once punched you so hard

in the thigh it left a bruise the size
and shape of the dark purple pansies

your mother planted each spring—
small purple flags to claim the soil

of a place she wasn't born into.
Slowly, the bruise grew a yellow halo,

and you were silent about that too,
until your mother found it in the bath.

The words that came then were hers,
fear that you understood only as anger—

Why didn't you tell?!—and a visit
to the teacher despite your pleas.

It wouldn't work, you knew.
That night, awake in the silent house,

you fingered the bruise and heard,
or thought you heard, a humming

that might have been a word.

Almost a Mothering

Consider reduction—the five turkey vultures
making sleek dark circles above the field

this morning. They hunt by smell, I read,
but *hunt* isn't right—instead they gather

from the air some wind-translated
sign of carcass. No punishment, nothing inflicted—

the angle of their plunge a means to rewind
body to material, almost a mothering.

Each afternoon, when the freight train
pushes its high whine

through the culvert near the field,
I remember I was named

for the woman in that famous Russian novel,
who tossed herself from the station platform

as the engine pulled in.
No revising that action.

She was a mother too.
At twelve, I read it and thought her a fool.

Now, I see how a life buckles—
a horse whose head has been yanked

too often takes command how it can.
The vultures land

in the lichened branches of a nearby tree,
to claim the offal of this neighborhood.

Red-crowned, they preen
with their hooked beaks, accepting every stain.

Self-Portrait as Smaller Moon

"The remnants of a second moon that orbited the Earth
billions of years ago may be splattered across the far side
of our moon, scientists claim . . . [T]he two appear to have
crunched together in a gentle collision."—*The Guardian*, 8/3/11

I wasn't looking at her.

Instead, I watched years of tides
dismantle coasts, watched my shadow
paint its pupil on revolving blue, watched haze,
watched birds, watched icecaps spread
and shrivel, but not the path I traced above
or who flew with me.

What is belonging?
I floated in my dust and ore,
collecting light like sympathy
from strangers, and when it came,
the wind felt this way too—polite intrusion.
Pay attention,

mothers say, *look both ways, don't
follow strangers.* But in that turning,
I forgot. Startled by this one
so close behind,
I wobbled toward her, heeling
before I knew I moved.

Where does the moon go, mama? I went
to mountains, foothills, craters,
spread myself against the dark back
of this lovely other, burrowed in,
as lighter rocks slipped singly by,
pursuing their own gravity.

Journey

Stunned, the pullets stand
inside their bright, new run.

They peck at specks of dirt
on the white frame.

One tries to gnaw a rung
of the ladder up

to their coop.
Can chickens gnaw?

They have no teeth.
But she takes it sideways

in her beak, experimentally,
as she eyes me.

What must it have been like
to leave the dark shed

of their hatching
and ride inside the heart

of a whirring, thudding animal
to arrive here

still, apparently, alive?
They shake their wings,

as if testing that feathers
can rise and catch the air

of this new atmosphere,
then try their small,

half-swallowed calls.
I could say it was like being born,

but who remembers that?
Neither me nor the hens,

one of whom now lifts
her red-combed head,

and hooks
a prehistoric three-toed foot

onto the ladder,
climbing it to the top.

Milk Teeth

After I lost the third—
the ultrasound a grainy, static blur—

a friend said I should try to foster,
said it wide-eyed from across

her holiday potluck table,
all those chewing mouths.

I couldn't speak,
suddenly able to see

myself a predicament, considered
like the lone loon on the lake upstate—

how would it survive itself?

Hadn't I tried, twice,
to go to the local animal shelter

just to look,
came back each time with a kitten

kneading my sweater for milk.
Once, I woke in the night

to teeth on my nipple,
gave it my littlest finger

to mouth instead,
but remembered the bite

years later, nursing my daughter
beneath the bedside light.

Self-Portrait with Alternate Ending

Keep 5:30, perfect June almost evening. Keep
forgetting dinner and walking out into the day exhaling
sweat, exhaust, and unseen sea like a lost gull.
Keep the mile-away bay we head for now,
the baby in her stroller, queen at ship's prow,
trying her new word—*kitty, kitty*—
on every moving thing. Keep *kitty, kitty*. Keep
the humped driveway that catches the stroller's wheels,
the cracked sidewalk and ragged curb,
where we stop to let three boys run past—
t-shirts flashing white. They don't turn to see us.
Keep the boys as we start out again to cross our street
and, *kitty, kitty*, keep three more boys running,
not so fast but tracking the first three. They stop
for us who have interrupted their game.
The tallest one—his red and white striped shirt,
his hand in his pocket. Keep the shirt,
keep the hand, not the pocket. Keep the movement
of his legs as he again begins to run,
keep the neighbor who calls to us as we cross over.
Keep the mother who is sitting home with supper,
or who is working in a hotel changing other people's sheets,
or who is pulling into her driveway and calling to her neighbor
Have you seen him?—her boy who stops now
to take the gun out of his pocket
to fire its *pop-pop-pop* at the other boys retreating,
their t-shirt flags waving—don't keep this.
And the unsound as it arcs, as it tunnels through the air,
or the whirring of the stroller's wheels as our legs unfurl—
no wall or open door, but endless pavement and a bullet
that is somewhere. Keep it somewhere,

somewhere fallen in the grass,
where later plainclothes cops will find it, reassure us
that we weren't *an intended target*. Take out target.
Take out intention. Keep the baby in her stroller
singing softer now her *kitty, kitty*
as we jolt home, the sky a mask behind us.

Back Porch Aubade

Through the highway's underlying monochord,
through gear-strain and down shift on avenues
marked with blue and white *Evacuation Route* signs
(a siren interrupts, then recedes),
through air brake release and city bus clutch at corners,
a slight hollow wooden mallet tremolo—*Tap-tap*.
It could be the neighbor's downspout
dripping to the gutter, but no, too rhythmic—
stopping and again starting as though
it's caught me catching it here, on the porch,
having just let our chickens out into the backyard,
yesterday's snow subsiding to rain,
and the buds on the apple trees surviving
despite late freeze. *Tap-tap*. I strain for it—
a second hand that records and then relents.
Is it in the elm grown thin with disease
or a street-leaning spruce? *Tap-tap*. My alarm
buzzes my hip, and inside the house
the kids need breakfast, shoes, coats
before we leave to meet the school bus
already shouldering its metronomic
warning lights through traffic toward our curb.
And how can there be chickens and apple trees
amid all this asphalt and combustion?
How can there be children, but there are, and also
on a storm-softened trunk somewhere nearby,
its quick bill pausing then resuming dissection
of bark and wood rot for ants or beetle larvae—anything
that moves or grows within it—a woodpecker.

Real Life

On our walk to the science museum,
my daughter spots a jet chalking its contrail on sky,

asks *how small did the people have to get to fit inside?*
And instead of trying to explain distance

or physics I only partly understand, I want
domino suitcases, toothbrushes the size of rice grains,

all of us reduced to our lightest, most exact selves.
But when we reach the museum's *Transportation* display

with its model trains and full-size climb-in replica
of the Apollo Lunar Module,

she tells me that *in real life*, planes are large enough
to let us step aboard without shrinking,

although later, in the halls of *Human Life*
and *Then and Now*, we agree it's difficult to tell

the long-ago real people from those they imagined
we might be, and *What color were their houses?*

Could we visit them if we walked or swam far enough?

Then, in *New England Habitats*, we find
two deer, legs splayed atop a concrete rock

next to a painted stream, and a nesting pair of grebes
with pieces of marsh grass decades in their beaks.

Across the hall, the lone moose hefts his many-fingered
rack expectantly, as if the next field trip train of kids

will be the one to lead him out, across Rt. 28
and down into the Charles, where the duck boats leave

diesel V's against the current.
In front of his case, there's a button we can press to know his scent—

sawdust mixed with the sour memory of meat—
is this to help us feel that he is real?

But now my daughter is leading me
to the gray wolf silent by the door,

her head lowered to sniff
the smoky blur of half-blind pups, who lift

fine-needled paws toward her dim light.

Arithmetic

White 1, yellow 5, red 10—at school,
my daughter's learning math with colored blocks.

She sorts and measures, measures and sorts—
How many ways to make a ten?—rewarding same

with same. On the rug, the children rush to say
that *she is five and so is he and she and she . . .*

all except the boy who's six
and wonders if he's turned another animal.

At home, my daughter says her skin is pale,
paler than mine, but mine is

*paler than Jasmin, who's paler than Jaziyah, who's paler
than Aniyah, who's paler than Laray, who's darkest of all.*

She pauses.
I watch her adding and subtracting.

Outside, some kids are kicking ball.
We hear them through the window—

the last few leaves gold on their branches,
the sky already softening towards dusk.

How many ways to make a ten.
The light comes in to us translucent, cool.

We sit here, figuring.

Causes Unknown

In the split between two boulders
behind the blue and orange playground,

the children are building nests
for when the hurricane comes.

Assembly line, they pass small piles of twigs
and—*Faster!*—last year's leaves,

then climb inside with larger sticks *for rowing.*
April now, and the last storm has redrawn

all the Atlantic flood maps. One more year
until the Cartaret Islands go down in the Pacific—

whole forests past all rowing.
One morning in December,

my friend will go in to wake her two-year-old son,
and find him.

Causes unknown, the doctors will say—
some stuttered synapse blanking.

What tide could bear this?
She'll write his obituary for the local news.

Is it tomorrow? my son asks at bedtime each night,
and in the morning asks again.

All Hallows

The year that she was three,
my daughter was a fox for Halloween—
orange felt hood with ears, a tail stitched
to her back, and painted-on whiskers—
the only girl in the preschool parade
not dressed as a princess.

That was the same year something
kept finding its way through the back wall
of Granny's garden to dig up moles.
Mornings, we'd find the excavated holes—
entrances we hadn't known existed.
A fox, said Mr. Lovely, who came to cut
the grass—we'd need to put down poison.
But would that remove the fox
or just the moles, we asked, and wouldn't it
be better to find the wall's gap and fill it?

My daughter cried for the fox
she never saw, begged us not to kill it.
But still she didn't want to go alone
into the garden.

I think now she was trying on fear
that Halloween—not the fox circling
the henhouse kind, but the unseen thing
that leaves a gash exposing mud and plunder
beneath the grass you thought you knew.
In the picture we took, I hold her
and her baby brother on my lap. He stares
at her strange ears and painted face, amazed.
She bares her teeth and locks the camera in her gaze.

Self-Portrait Without Wings

You get them in middle school,
I heard a fifth-grade girl say at the bus stop.
But middle school girls rode a different bus,
so I couldn't check. Sometimes we'd pass one
waiting at her stop, and I'd squint to see—
something pulling at the shoulders of her uniform,
loosening along her spine?
I was never close enough.

The milk at school tasted sharp,
like the edges of the thick white paper
Ms. Kempe gave us for portraits of trees.
I only had room for the trunks.

Riding home, I'd kneel on the green vinyl seat to watch.
Something about the way those girls walked—
backpacks hunched, dark blue skirts unpleating in the wind
as they leaned toward the bells of their shadows.
The white dashes on the road blurred into a long gray stripe
and suddenly we were rising in one large flock—
school sweaters, skirts, and buckle shoes falling
through the bare branches below.

Passenger Pigeon

I read once that they traveled
in flocks big as hurricanes, and as fast—
millions of birds flying so low
you almost didn't need a gun to catch
one, just reach an arm up and grab.
Too easy, nuisance birds, landing
and deflowering a tree or field
in minutes, then lolling around,
dirtying the ground, before the swift,
swirling rise toward elsewhere.
Who was their passenger?
Or is passage the important part—
the routes they moved through air.
We care so much about who
belongs where, arm ourselves
against the imaginary. No one
believed they could die out.
There were so many.

What is the Poem

Is it an apparition, a machine of memory,
or the story of remembering?

This one begins in summer
with a girl alone in her room

changing out of her bathing suit—
the damp polyester sucking down

her flat girl chest, barely needing to stretch
over the slight flare of hips and pelvis

and thighs to slide past her calves to the floor.
It continues when her cousin slams open the door.

It continues when he pins her silent to the bed
and pries her fingers, one by one,

and then each thumb from what
she tries to hide, then stretches wide

her arms and legs to look
at all the places the bathing suit has touched.

What happened next?
Did a voice in the hall intervene?

Was he afraid I'd remember my own and scream?
The poem doesn't know why he let go, leaving

the door flapping after him,
useless as a single wing.

And the grown-ups in the kitchen didn't ask—
Just kids—when I ran past

and out to the yard's dry grass.
But by then there was an order

to things, a door the poem keeps forcing
open as I twist my shoulders

back into the bathing suit's straps,
lifting them up and over, up and over.

Fugue

Can you tell us what you don't forget?
the senator's voice repeats
from the radio. It's rush hour, Boston, I-93,

driving home from dance class
with my daughter in the back seat,
her twelve-year-old legs stretched

long in pink Body Wrappers brand spandex
as she wonders aloud what we're going to eat
for dinner. Air brakes wheeze, then release

beside us as a bus muscles past,
and should I change the station
as the senator's voice repeats

Can you tell us what you don't forget?
above the traffic—rush hour, Boston, I-93,
my daughter in the back seat—

girl whose body I once unwrapped from mine,
is she listening as now the woman speaks?
I was pushed onto the bed.

His weight was heavy.
I shake my head—
Boston, rush hour, I-93—

as if I could swerve by what edges up in me.
He put his hand over my mouth.
It was hard for me to breathe.

Boston, rush hour, I-93,
but I'm cruising a suburban street
of dandelion lawns, legs the same age

as my daughter, who jams her knees
against my seat when I hit the brakes
as one last car squeezes ahead of me.

Can you tell us

Boston, rush hour. I-93
is fixed to a grid of red

what you don't forget?

taillights that bleed
their afterimages

Can you

against gray sky.
I'm tired,

forget

picturing my bed back home

what you don't

quilt pulled tight
against the sheets

Can you   don't   forget

or is it that other bed

what you

and what year was it

forget   don't

what day

don't   Can you   forget

how

tell us   don't   tell   what

did he

                                     what   *Can you*   *forget*   *don't*   *tell us*

touch me?

      I was wearing a one-piece bathing suit.
      I believed
      he was going to rape me.

Boston, rush hour, I-93,
a tail light flickers, horns begin to beep,
How many times will I repeat

this drive?
      Mom? When are we going to move?
Her voice reaches toward me, and I ease

my weight up off the brake,
considering the question. The miles, like bodies,
fall between us and what I don't forget

in Boston, rush hour, I-93,
driving home from dance class
with my daughter in the back seat.

Not if, but when,

the scientists all agreed, when the news ran
the picture of the man on his paddle board,

a great white trailing silently behind
just feet from the beach, kids and seals

splashing in the surf. So next day
I'm the embarrassing stranger lady

wading toward the four tween boys
with their boogie boards,

un-sunned arm pointing to the posted warning:
Be shark smart: don't swim near seals!

I look for mothers, wonder if they mind
me worrying the boys—my own daughter,

just their age, safe at home, inland.
These days she can spend hours looking

as new shapes emerge in the mirror:
lengthening thigh rounding to hip, swell

of collarbone buoying neck,
cheek cresting beneath her gaze.

How easy to make a mistake,
find herself alone one dawn or dusk

following a warming current out
past where her feet can touch,

something unseen hungering near.
And those boys on the beach,

who's teaching them the signs:
shiny hook, bare skin, deep water

funneling one uncertain shape toward another.
Not if—but when.

Knees grazing sand, I swim the shallows
parallel to shore, calculating:

The one who held me down.
The one who pressed himself sharp

into me on the rush hour train.
The one who forced a kiss on the bus

and the other riders' laughter.
The one who grabbed me from behind

in the dark bar.
The one I bled after.

At home, my daughter's reflection
stares at her from the bathroom door,

but soon she'll open it, step out,
and what wave will greet her then,

sweeping her beyond me in its net of salt?
I paddle back to where I've left my things,

watching for boys and seals,
but now the August sun is going down,

and they and whatever led them here
have disappeared.

Thirteen

Here's to the beautiful daughters
who eat all the cookies
who won't sleep and don't sleep and then sleep
all Saturday until hunger engines them up
into the noon kitchen glowering.
Who snatch our good red boots,
colting down the hall, out the door
in our new black sweater. Who grow.
Who grow.
Who smile silent out the backseat window
all throughout the *hello* and *how was* and *did you*
and *I did* and *and, and, and* . . . monologue—
who are they looking at?
Who freckle and tangle,
Sturm und Drang,
blame and are right
and still want a song at good night.
Who ask.
Who ask and the answer is no, is yes.
Who ask and the answers skein philosophical,
barbed, skinless, capillary.
Who ask and remind us.
Who know the inside of us.
Who don't remember, who do.
Who get and give.
Who live.
Who forgive.

Self-Portrait at Tree Line

My body moves ahead of me
into underbrush. Hum of engine or sky behind,

and something that is not love
closes the roads and locks its doors. I am shadow,

fern, ripple, as I move upward through satellite crackle
and oxygen rush—the breaking news of myself—

to where these trunks of wind-cured pines
cast blue shade against white ice. Beyond prey

and preyed upon, what is this light like,
if it is light at all and not exit?

I think I would crouch here,
in the space between shelter and peak,

but the pelt of me feels voices in the foothills,
and a metal song of bullet threads the air.

Explaining Tampons to My Son

Mama, what are those? he asks,
pointing to the small cardboard box that
appears monthly on the toilet tank. So I tell him
inside . . . uterus . . . a baby could grow . . . doesn't.
Serious-eyed, he listens.
Don't worry, it doesn't hurt, I lie.
No baby? he says. *Yes, Baby,* I nod, *no baby.*
We've been reading Greek myths—
the gods swallowing their children
or hiding them away in caves,
Zeus ravishing women into cows
and islands and ash (Did it hurt?),
Hera fuming, the other Olympians
gorgeous on their thrones,
trying to get one over on each other
on earth. No blood, but ichor,
and ambrosia to smooth their battle nicks.
I think of washing my sheets this morning,
generations of smiling TV women in my head
calmly conquering grass stains, grease,
mud, blood—the *dried in* and *caked on.*
Back on the couch, he leans close,
squeezing himself against me. *Keep reading.*
We've reached Troy—a whole city
and so many favored heroes demolished
over a goddess snit fit and a greedy boy—
before the Romans take over, with their temples
not so beautiful, but more luxurious.
What's "luxurious"? he asks.
Expensive, I tell him, *something everyone wants.*
But not beautiful? he asks. *Maybe not.*

This is confusing. *Also comfortable*, I say.
It's the end of the story now—
all the gods renamed, then given up
to constellations almost obscured
by light pollution and bedtime schedules.
Mama, have you finished shedding your blood?
he asks after brushing his teeth.
Mostly, I say. He nods, burrowing down
into the luxury of his bed.

Wrestling With Gods

"After every war someone has to tidy up."
—*Wisława Szymborska*

You are in the small tornado of your own element!
my son shouts from the living room couch,
instructing his father on their next battle.

No, no, like this—thwack of cushions—*I win!*
Narrative is important, also the rules—
who decides the terrain, personnel,

weapons, size of the tornado.
Yesterday, it was cheetah vs. tiger
and my abdomen he rammed first

with a pillow, then his head, as if trying to reverse
the last seven years. Other days,
it's Thor and Loki or Zeus and Apollo.

Each time, I brace myself into a tripod
on my knees wondering what we're preparing for,
as he storms across the practical, all-weather upholstery.

Today, on the kitchen radio, a BBC reporter
somewhere near the Syrian border responds
We understand that this may be a very dynamic war

to a question I didn't hear.
I had to train myself to wrestle, learn
not to flinch as my son dove toward muscles

he once stretched, jabbing from within.
We practice battles already knowing the endings—
You be Achilles and I'll be Thetis,

wringing the hand that held her boy's naked
tendon as the president's helicopter retreats
over the sea. Now, in the living room,

my son growls and tucks his chin
as he becomes a Spinosaurus.
My husband turns into a killer octopus,

and the BBC moves to a new headline
on a different continent.
I steady myself

against the granite lip of the kitchen sink,
its crystals volcanic,
all that heat turned element.

At North

On my laptop screen, the blunt boat's prow
presses blue cracks into white ice
like a stick figure chalked onto snow.

Ahead, the Pole shifts amid the ridges.

I imagine it while watering the backyard chickens,
hear it in the kitchen tap drip after rinsing the dishes,
think of a compass whirling while steering the evening carpool home.

Up there, the light slides white into white, on or out.

I imagine seals hemming the green-dark waves
and bears hunched huge as they stalk
the thinning floes.

        My children play *Boats and Islands* in the bath.

I imagine myself as a speck of heat, a retinal trick
moving across the blank cap,
an idea that floats and drifts—

an unstationary station.

        My children play *School* in the living room.
        They sing a song about continents.

I scroll down.

On the next screen, a boy has entered a building.
On the next screen a chain of students following each other
out of the building.

> My children play *Containment Drill* in their bedroom
> The rules are *turn out the lights, shut the door,*
> *sit on the rug and wait.*

The students raise their arms in the air,
then put them down. They don't know where
to put their arms.

> My children sit quietly.
> The bears have been swimming a long time.

Everything but the sea contracts.

Pastoral

Alarm call of gull in the Ikea parking garage,
and I turn, expecting claws, to find only beams

and ceiling pipes. Then a starling screams
by the red-lit E of the entrance sign, but no wing startles,

and as the gull circles once more,
I hear it for what it is—a loop to scare other birds

from settling their mess of sticks and straw
in this concrete box store built on drained swamp.

We load our packages into the hatchback
and follow signs out to the highway, where hawks—

real ones—roost in the verges,
on our way back home, where you'll make the coffee

and I'll scan the latest headlines and ads
for *Bulletproof School Supplies* and *Bodyguard Blankets.*

In the pictures, rows of six-year-olds hunch
beneath tunnels of bright red padded mats

just like the Greeks and Romans once locked their shields,
a company exec explains. My coffee's cold,

our discount furniture, still packed, is stacked
against the wall, as bird cries accumulate in sky

above our yard. It's nearly time to walk outside
to meet the flocks of black and yellow

school buses returning down our street,
make dinner, call the kids in to eat.

She threw herself
upon the coffin

as it moved down the nave
on silent, wheeled hydraulics
so that the pall-bearers—tall boys
like him—did not bear but steered it
like an awkward boat without a prow,
like nothing but a coffin, really,
raised on a cart to glide eye-level
past the pews, and when it passed,
she threw herself upon it—
first her hands, then lowering
her forearms down against
the varnished metal finish, she pushed
until her torso lay along the curving
lid, across the place where his
might lie below it, then lay
her head above his head
that years before was lidded
by her skin, boy head she carried,
covered, washed, and woke,
and rubbed and combed and chased
to bed and warned and kissed
as she does now the spot she's thrown
herself upon, upon the coffin
of the one the papers labeled *man*,
as in *a man was shot and killed Tuesday*,
though he was only weeks past twenty-one,
not son, not name, not love, but *man*,
as though the bullet made him whole
and finished him,
but not for her, who lay now on the coffin,
unfinished and undone, as if she could

undo the night, the car, the friend
who wouldn't speak, the shots
the neighbors thought were fireworks,
the evidence markers visible on the street—
all of it she threw herself upon, and also
on the coffin holding the body of her son,
as we all watched, and could not
move or speak, as if the air we would
have used to do those things was gone.

Self-Portrait with Refrain

Every day, your children go to school.
It is a beautiful school—red brick upon a hill,
with windows that face out to sea—
your son's classroom on the bottom floor,
your daughter's on the second.
From her square table, she can see
the harbor islands humped like animals asleep
within the bay, the train line running along shore.

Every day, you take that train to work.
Whatever you are doing as you ride—
talking, reading, scanning your phone for news—
you look up as the school comes into view.
You look up to your son on the bottom floor,
your daughter on the second.

Every day, your children go to school.
Every day, passing below, you look up
and think of the heavy, steel front door
that clicks when it locks behind their backs
each morning as they go into the school.
You think of other doors—one opens
on the basketball court, two more
on the asphalt lot behind the school
where parents collect in the afternoon,
one opens to your son's class
on the bottom floor.

Every day, your children go to school,
and every day, you think of the doors.

You think of the boy or man
who holds something in his hand
as he tries the locked front door.
You think of him turning,
careful, the object pressed to his chest,
and walking to the basketball court door.
Why do you think of him?
Mid-morning, and the sun finds his white hands,
finds the faded orange rim of the hoop,
finds the muzzle's matte black curve
as he moves to check the locked back doors
one by one.

It is a lovely day, this day
when your children go to school.
Spring, with a slight breeze from the sea—
why not leave the door open to it,
your son's teacher thinks, so the breeze can reach
the children on their mats at rest time.

I never sleep at rest time, your son declares,
and so, lying awake on his robot sheets,
he sees the man enter the room,
sees the thing in his hands almost familiar—
like the one great-grandma sent at Christmas,
but not red and blue, and what comes out
is not rubber balls.

Why think of this?
Why wonder if your daughter,
on the second floor of the beautiful school

with windows that look out to sea,
recognizes gunfire in the noise
two floors below. Does she hear
no more fighting over who got the bigger bowl,
all the world of ice cream now hers alone,
the known night tides of breath and shift
erased from the bottom bunk.

Every day, your children go to school,
the same school high upon the hill.
Every day, you take the train, passing too far away
to hear if there is silence
in the room on the second floor,
the drill practiced so often—lock the door,
sit on the rug, pretend you aren't there.
From each window, the harbor islands flicker
a hide and seek of wave and heat.

But why think of this? Every day,
the children waiting, and you
too far away to hear?
The shuddering train that draws you on
like sand a wave pulls back to sea—
you look up from your book in time to see
the open door, the sirens gathering.

Every day, your children go to school,
Every day, you pass below,
too far away to hear, and look up—
who is that standing in the doorway?
Why must you think of this?

The train picking up speed now,
soon entering the tunnel where you'll lose
sight of the beautiful building—red brick, upon a hill,
with windows that face out to sea,
where, every day, your children go to school.

Utility Report

All night, the gas company backhoe idles
outside the house—melisma of engine punctured

by the pure tone beep of the back-up alarm.
Gas in the manhole, the foreman in yellow Hi-Viz vest

shouts, leaning down from the lit cab of his truck.
By morning, the dark hole in the pavement

has gathered foothills of mud and gravel.
The men stand around and look down.

One lowers a long blue tube into it,
while I pack school lunches in the kitchen,

then turn on the news to check the *World Update*:
Merkel condemns closure of Balkan route . . .

(blast of jackhammer from the street outside)
Austria, Slovenia, Croatia, Serbia, and Macedonia

have all acted to stem the migrant flow. The camera zooms
to a Gore-Texed reporter standing at the border.

Behind him, two kids photo-bomb the shot,
peek-a-booing from the mouth of their army green tent.

Nothing's blowing up, ma'am, the foreman laughed
when I asked should I wake my kids, move them

from their rooms at the front of the house?
But we know gas follows the path of least resistance—

seal one crack, it finds another farther on.
The camera shifts to a different camp

where police in mirrored masks *accomplish clearance,*
demolition, dispersal. Outside, the workmen

study their pipe and tunnel, fill their hole,
and move on to the next point of detection,

leaving behind a crumpled orange safety cone
on the dust-smeared square of road.

The Crossing

In this morning's paper, a story of thirteen women
drowned off the coast of Lampedusa—
heavy weather, the ship found *listing*.
When the rescue vessels heard
the distress call, they hurried toward it.
And when the *migrants*—this is the name
the Italian Coast Guard gave the women,
the eight-month-old baby, and nearly fifty others
drifting with them on the water's skin
for days (the paper doesn't say how many)—
when the *migrants* saw hope approaching,
motoring across what had been empty waves,
they rushed together to meet it.
It was this *sudden movement* (the paper says)
that lifted the boat sideways
like a hand raised in greeting,
so that the people—let's name them people,
those sisters, mothers, children—
slid quickly from its palm into the water,
which they found opened to them after all,
yielding like an unlatched gate to their fall,
and then behind them closing.

Studies Show

Afternoons, the hens scratch dust baths
in the loose dirt near the dogwood tree—
shallow ovals they deflate into,

heads slumped to one side,
as if some large animal had moved through,
puncturing them all.

Then a flutter of wing showers
fine brown powder, and the backyard fills
with resurrection, a surprise every time.

Humans, studies show, are terrible
at calculating risk, unable to resist
appearances—the hens felled by plague,

not preening. Or do we need to believe
the calm morning sea immune to storm?
Last week, over one thousand drowned,

crossing from one country to another—
a passage they thought safe?
But safety is a rubber boat on a beach

when all that's behind you drones and collapses.
One thousand.
Gone from breakfast tables, beds.

No letters back.
But studies show large numbers are difficult
for humans to conceive. We need the particular

toddler collapsed on shore.
It's May. I wear a shirt almost as pink
as the dogwood's blossoms,

same foolish pink as the one I wore
the day my waters broke, and I became
my daughter's failing boat.

How many years since then,
and still I count the hens each morning
when I go out to feed them—

necks stretched like the prows
of miniature Phoenician ships as they plow
toward me. All beak and risk, no calculation.

Not Near, But Far

New to the city, I woke to blue,
blue filling my window's upper panes,
outlining rows of brick apartments
and the Gothic tower of Riverside Church
up the block—steel-framed,
I'd read, to sustain such weight—blue a stain
reaching into every surface.

I wanted coffee, thought I'd take a walk,
turned on the radio to screaming—*A plane! Another plane!*

On 125th street, the bars all stayed open.
We watched the ash accumulate on screens
above glowing rows of bottles—
the towers crumpling, then reassembling,
then crumpling again.

I wasn't near, I told Beth when she called from Boston.
Yes, you are! her voiced lunged toward me
through the wire. But we were far,
farther than we'd ever been before,
the buildings quiet now, the blue all gone.

Geography Report

In the locker room of the YMCA pool,
my daughter—skinny-limbed ten-year-old
in blue green swimsuit—
presses one sharp finger
into the loose skin below my navel,
laughing to see the white indented moon
she leaves there.

> From high enough, one body
> looks like any other—ten-year-old girl
> collecting firewood or man with gun—
> the coordinates close and closing
> in Laghman Province, Afghanistan.

From the pool's deck, I watch my daughter
kick and bob in chlorine blue,
torso and legs a momentary T
against the black spine of the lane
wavering beneath.

> *. . . solely with the intent of countering known insurgents,*
> the NATO spokesman speaks,
> as the girl's body bends—
> a piece of white cloth fluttering—
> then straightens holding a stick.

In the pool, my daughter rolls
and thrashes—element within element—
elbow flashing in air before it falls
then reappears—*Watch me!*

Is this a day the girl has waited for—
old enough now to work,
aunts, grandmother, the cousin married this spring
all nodding to her in the beginning light
of the hour before the early walk to school
(Is there a school?),
their bundles of brush stacked neatly
as the planes *engage with precision munitions*
and direct fire.

hip, flank,
shoulder at the water's lip—
Watch!—white flutter, kick
above the center line—
An arm crooks out, her fingers splayed,
each tendon raised and seeking
as she reaches for the wall.

Or would she have slept,
small moon beneath her blanket—
Unfortunately, we have become aware
of possible civilians—
let someone else walk out into the still-dark
morning, someone else
search out the branches to burn that hour.

Self-Portrait as Invasive Species

In the Viking room
of the National Archeology Museum
in Dublin, a glass case holds a child's leather boot.
Blackened but intact, with two soft flaps
to wrap the ankle of a toddler,
it sits between two knife sheaths
in its numbered spot: *10th Century, A.D.,*
Likely the son or daughter of a wealthy trader
(the poor wore wood), *discovered*
under High Street, Christchurch, Dublin.
Nearby, a model of their mud and wattle
settlement within palisades,
sharp under the Museum's LED lights.
Pails, cups, spoons, and mortars,
toy sword and model boats,
blacksmith tools, carved rings
and pendants from an amber worker's
house found beneath Fishamble Street,
a spindle whorl and three bone pins
like fingers! my daughter cried,
wanting to know if there were a *real skeleton*
in the Viking coffin, boat-shaped,
by the wall. But I thought of gardens—
what adopted shrub or flower
would these intruders, traders
who stayed long past trade,
have counted on to signal spring?
And then my mother, who one May day
flew out from here, leaving (she thought)
the crush of family—ten siblings,

a father drunk with Church.
No way for her to see the hull-shaped shadow
of her plane cutting irreversible
across Atlantic waves towards husband,
house, three daughters foreign-born,
and all our toys and tools—
those plastic boats and rubber boots
so permanently new.

Fence

(Amherst, VA)

Four strands of barbed wire strung
from thin brown metals posts that blend

into a field of ragweed, goldenrod, bluestem.
Beyond is sycamore and sky, where turkey vultures roost

and fly. Now, a man appears, walking the other side—
hard hat, a plastic jug strapped to his back,

spray hose draped across his chest.
Glancing up, he sees me seeing him.

Two more men follow, each carrying an axe.
One says something to the other—I catch

the open *ah* of Spanish vowels. Later, I go looking,
find the place where they've slid under—

the grass tamped to a brief hollow—
then hear them singing beyond a hedge, and see their truck

parked by the cut where the train tracks run.
They must be clearing them of kudzu—*miracle vine*

imported to save the soil of the Depression South,
renamed *invasive*, snake-filled monster,

still it grows on sunny rail banks
and the sides of roads. I think of the train

my great-grandfather rode north from Mexico City
alongside soldiers home from the Great War

and the flu that traveled with them.
It was 1918 when they crossed the border.

When my abuela and her mother followed
to bury him, was there a fence dividing

one story from another—
no more a wealthy farmer's daughter,

but the child of a single mother
living scared in a country where she didn't know

the language? Until the next war came,
and someone else became the other.

Back at my window, I watch
a frantic hummingbird inspect a flowering stalk—

marestail, or Canadian horseweed—
growing in a pot I once planted with petunias.

The fence wires shiver, then are still.
In the distance, a train is passing,

but by now the men with their axes
and their songs have moved on.

Hypothesis

Suppose you give up fear.

Suppose you go out into the back yard
white with the first snow of the year
and let the five black hens,
who press their cluster of spiky red combs
against the chain link gate, out of their pen,
knowing that somewhere nearby
the sharp-shinned hawk is circling.
The iridescent green on their feathers
flares in reflected snow light.
From inside the house, you watch
as they go about their scratching,
quick-beaked, in the bare earth
beneath the hydrangea sheltered
by the eaves of the garage.

Suppose that later, when a phone call
or some kitchen task has distracted you,
you hear the first chitter of their alarm
gutter, then rise. You open the back door
in time to see the unmistakable white
and brown-flecked breast, the curved,
attentive head and dark-backed wings
of the hawk as it lifts off the porch railing.

Suppose its claws are closed.
In the kitchen behind you, the radio denounces.
People are marching, have marched, will.
You hear them.

Suppose you give up fear.

Beneath the porch, the five hens
turn their heads toward you—
first one eye, then the other.
They ruffle gusts of flakes
as you herd them back into the pen.
There, in the laying box, you find
two brown eggs, smooth and almost warm,
which you carry, one in each hand,
back inside the house.

After All

Even when the garlic crop is good,
something else is always dying—

the peas withering in the afternoon we hoped
for rain instead of watering, the tomatoes

over-shaded. It should teach us something
about pathos or fate, but really

couldn't we have tried harder? Predicted
the week of heat when the spinach bolted?

The trouble with gardening
is there's rain and wind and sun to blame,

like the woman in the buffer zone
outside the clinic who spat at me and screamed

What kind of man is he to bring you here?
while I held your hand, and our daughter curled

in her crib at home with the sitter.
Afterward, I dozed against you

on a park bench overlooking the city
until I was ready to go back to work.

But that's not gardening.
And still there's the garlic—

those round, paper-skinned heads
you pulled this morning and carefully laid out

to dry on the driveway's warm flat bed
below our window.

The Naturalist's Report

We must keep energy moving through the system,
he repeats, pollen and cottonwood tracing
his hands in air. You look up into a Jeffrey pine

tall as a century, its long needles splayed
like the tines of many small rakes. When they drop,
they form jagged stacks that burn fast as a fire moves through,

sparing the trunk. *Fire is decomposition*—a way of making
room. You think of bodies made and unmade
within you—the ones who found breath,

the ones who never knew the place they'd left.
Like the lodgepole pines that have perfected leaving—
growing thin and close, so flames take them quickly,

scorching open their sealed cones
to let the seeds fall first to charcoal earth.

Self-Portrait as Fox in Daylight

I should be darkness, twitch of haunch,
and rumor among brush,

should skulk and den where my blue-eyed kits
burrow themselves in sleep,

should not be walking this road's tar
parade, its swindling itch

of light. I trouble
a nearby scent of mouse or vole,

then sit and stretch, then rise
to trot the double lines,

my tail a flare
to puzzled honks and rear-view stares.

I shuffle on—the heat a fence
I follow. How to explain?

I've been unmasked by sun,
its bitter yellow reach

that pins me sure as want
or stone to this bald stage.

I've lost the trick of you, my shade.

My son hands me the
Family Letter About This Unit

page torn from his fourth grade math book.
I'm supposed to read it, considering

how *geometry* and *classifying shapes*—
some words are highlighted so I get the gist—

might fit into dinner table chat or fights
about whose turn it is to take a bath first tonight.

I misread *convert* as covert and lose minutes
wondering what a covert measurement could be,

and why. But no one wants to know
they're being measured or tested, do they?

Even though we are every day—
all our angry faces, likes, and hearts totted up,

politicians and yoghurts we prefer,
a pointillist scrim gluing us to the world,

little sticky bits tracing wherever we've been.
But maybe I should say *I* not *we*:

I don't like being tested.
My husband, for instance, doesn't seem to mind—

almost high school dropout with a perfect score
on his SAT. But all those choices freeze me.

The *Family Letter* tells me I should
encourage your child to explain.

True or False: I am a good mother
if I am always awake and dressed before my children.

True or False: I am a bad mother.
If I give up _____and start _____ing

three to five times a week, I am a good mother/wife/other.
Please identify my lines of symmetry.

But in high school, I liked geometry,
maybe because my teacher drove a sky blue Corvette

and wore vintage polyester skirt suits
and maybe because the tests felt like stories

of how one shape could become another,
divided but still itself.

I liked that I could see it happening, point
by point, the way every night,

after my husband and the kids are asleep,
I go around the house clicking off each light

until I become invisible, even to myself.

The Algorithm Thinks I Need a Girdle

"Are you ready to fall in love?"
—*Shapermint.com*

O, to *forget heartbreaking panty lines*,
take heart and step out,
following lines panting in the mind,
to get and get gone and find
gravity's brake, to bind
hip, thigh, waist, to bone
while the crowd scrolls by on *dig free legs*,
ring lights lit, filters aligned,
as the nerve knives strobe through,
unfree of body unsoothed,
as O, the mouth rounds the vowel
dug free from throat, and who
wouldn't want *full body smoothing
love in seconds*, O algorithm
honing your philosophy of lack,
who could refuse such promises—
a garment *to keep everything where it needs to be*,
O need, O keep, O thing, O be,
O you, smoothing your way through
those every bodies towards mine,
each second realigning me for
love, in its *instant shaping power*.

Heaven Knows

Some days, you wake up
and the light in the field is like swimming

or moving through clear fog, is something that pushes
back—not startling but steady pressure,

the wall-to-wall world cruising your skin.
Up ahead, a goldfinch flickers, and what is it

that you can't remember? The years ago *No!*
you said to that boy in a Dublin bar

before stumbling down a flight of stairs to be sick,
the slick surface of the bathroom mirror

slapping you back from the brink
of a different bed in a different country

(just like your mother chose)? But why
should it always revolve around a man?

What about the aria you could've sung louder
at the audition, the letter from a famous poet

you never answered? Maybe the garage
would be less cluttered with broken sleds

and old TV sets, the workbench a sinkhole
of socket wrenches and drill bits. Maybe

you'd be a neurosurgeon with a yacht
and a coke habit you're thinking you should quit,

but not yet. Maybe your mother would be happy
she'd left home. Maybe she'd stop calling you

the reason she could never go back.
Maybe not.

Behind the barn, the grain silos rise,
gray columns braceleted by darker iron rebar

like the necks of enormous, rust-streaked
prehistoric birds. The grass around them

needs mowing, but now it's starting to rain.
You should have known that would happen.

Self-Portrait Instead of Engine

Not the tracks or the horn,
not the cable's grease and spark
not the bold-print charts of approach

and departure. Not the steam,
or electricity running
fast and straight as a child

whose mother has just turned
her back. Not the bridges,
the platforms like redemption,

or the walls—pocked concrete tiles
that promise you can keep out
the noise—No,

not the fences, or the yards—
some ordered green,
sprawl of trikes and plastic cars

in others.
But perhaps marsh grass
as it crowds the causeways,

the waters beyond in tantrum
and sleep always touching
shore. Or rain—

rain like rain only—
playing the roof all through
afternoon and then night.

At Collinsville Bridge

We knew the bridge before we knew it:
rusted X of girders a diagram of long gone
warehouse and railroad. Knew if we could master
the sixty-foot wingspan of its drop into the lap
of water loose against bank, we would know
something better. *Aim for my wake*, you said—

a bullseye pupil dilating. We were not our mothers
yet, and so could hold the story of that boy who jumped
too late last August and found the rapids a thin cloth
on a rocky table that broke his fall as proof of luck—
not his, but ours to straddle along with the iron rail
before we unfastened ourselves to fly.

Self-Portrait with Washing Machine

In those days, children slept all over us,
and we were fast and best, but didn't know it,
and sticky and milk-sour, and they were perfect pink mouths
of unknowing, each breath filling theirs with ours.
The children slept, and we slept, and we were happy.
And when we woke we learned about choices we'd been making
when we thought we were putting on our good shoes
(the ones our mothers gave us), or missing the last bus back,
or wondering if we really liked cilantro after all
(its sweet rot smell), or letting a boy show us mountains
from the window of a plane. But no, they were choices,
and here were new small bodies to prove it.
So we slept and woke to stand facing the washing machine
and chose warm, chose cold, chose permanent press
with medium spin express wash normal/casual.
We spun the dial and rinsed where it landed,
and we were happy, and then we slept.
And when we woke we saw figures walking
through the trees in the park across the street.
They stopped (their bodies momentary trunks)
and then kept moving, and we were happy.
And on the parent and child parking signs at the grocery store
we were a tall triangle with a circle head bending down
to a short square with a circle head looking up.
And we slept. And we were happy.
And the children woke to tell us a new age had come
into their bodies, that they could feel it beating,
and we were happy, and we slept. And the children woke,
and we tried to explain the difference
between *country* (was there a wall over the mountains?)
and *city* and *here*, each a shape falling smaller inside another.

And we slept. And the children woke. And we woke.
And we reminded ourselves to wash the strawberries
in vinegar so they wouldn't spoil, and pack the lunches
(choosing the fruit piece by piece into plastic snap-lid boxes),
and hang the clothes to dry, and we were happy,
and we slept, and the thing that
was happy slept too.

One Time

She left for good one time
but came back.
She let her hair grow long
and the grays come in.
Nobody ever asked about it,
but she left for good one time.
She followed the fence line out,
the grass dry and rust-tipped
where it chased her calves.
She was wearing the wrong shoes
and no socks either, but she'd left,
and it was for good.
Two does started from their beds
under a chokecherry. They cleared
the top wire of the fence
almost before she'd seen them
and kept moving into the trees
by the ditch. She was going
and she was gone, mosquitos
tracking her shoulder blades,
ringing her ankles. She kept
the fence line to her left
and the creek to her right as she left
(for good, for better or worse)
the dishes and whatever had been said
at dinner—the whole damn dinner!
She was leaving, she was
and was and was, the smell of her
falling under sagebrush, no wind yet,
and the sun not down.
You'll take what God gives you, they said,

as her children wriggled beside her
and the last bite on her plate
gave her the fisheye.
But she'd left for good,
and the creek agreed, flashing
the last acre until it slid
under the single barbed strand
that marked the neighbor's land,
and someone else called
someone else in to supper.
It would be bedtime soon,
the nighthawks buzzing the trees
for insects, their chicks
lodged among river stones below.
It had been for good when she left,
all of it, she knew, and also
that someone would need
a last drink of water now,
and a song *from when you were little*.
Someone would need
to touch her hair, to pat it softly
until sleep came this time,
and for good.

Notes

P. 13 In "Anxious Talker," the line "There is a place where words are born of silence" is from the poem "The Beloved" by Rumi, from *In the Arms of the Beloved*, translated by Jonathan Star.

P. 25 "Real Life" references the titles of museum exhibits at the Museum of Science, Boston.

P. 37 "Fugue" uses quotes from the transcript, as published in *The Washington Post*, of Dr. Christine Blasey Ford's testimony during the "Senate Judiciary Committee Hearing on the Nomination of Brett M. Kavanaugh to be an Associate Justice of the Supreme Court, Day 5, Focusing on Allegations of Sexual Assault." It specifically quotes Senator Amy Klobuchar's question to Dr. Ford and Dr. Ford's response, in part. (https://www.washingtonpost.com/news/national/wp/2018/09/27/kavanaugh-hearing-transcript/)

P. 40 *"Not if, but when,"* references drone photos taken by Cody DeGroff of a great white shark and paddleboarder Roger Freeman just north of Nauset Beach, Cape Cod. (https://boston.cbslocal.com/2018/07/30/paddleboarder-has-close-encounter-with-shark-on-cape-cod/)

P. 45 "Explaining Tampons to My Son" quotes language from *D'Aulaire's Book of Greek Myths* by Ingri and Edgar Parin D'Aulaire

P. 51 "Pastoral" quotes advertising copy for the Bodyguard Blanket from ProTecht, a now-defunct protective and safety products company in Oklahoma.

P. 53 "She threw herself upon the coffin" is for Elizabeth Cardoso and in memory of Jonathan Cardoso. It contains quoted language from *The Boston Globe* article "Man is killed in Dorchester shooting" by Travis Anderson, Globe Staff, September 21, 2016.

P. 61 "Utility Report" quotes language from "Migrant crisis: Angela Merkel condemns closure of Balkan route," *BBC News*, March 10, 2016 (https://www.bbc.com/news/world-europe-35772206)

P. 63 "The Crossing" contains quoted language from the *New York Times* article "Migrant Boat Capsizes Near Italy, Killing at Least 13 Women," by Reuters, October 7, 2019.

P. 67 "Geography Report" uses language from the articles "Karzai Denounces Coalition Over Airstikes" (Matthew Rosenberg, *New York Times*, Sept. 16, 2012) and "NATO disasters stack up in Afghanistan (Laura King, *Los Angeles Times*, September 16, 2012).

P. 81 "My son hands me the *Family Letter About This Unit*" quotes language from the TERC Investigations math curriculum "Unit 4: Measuring and Classifying Shapes."

P. 83 "The Algorithm Thinks I Need a Girdle" quotes advertising copy from Shapermint.com.

P. 84 "Heaven Knows" is written in response to Shelly Julian Bunde's painting "This is Dennis Rustad's niece from Pillsbury, North Dakota. Heaven knows how she got left to sort through the stuff and deal with the farm." 2013, acrylic and mixed media on wood panel.

P. 90 "One Time" is written in response to Shelly Julian Bunde's painting "This is Mrs. Lawrence Schlegel from outside of Hettinger, North Dakota. She left for good one time but came back. Nobody ever asked about it." 2013, acrylic on wood panel.

Biographical Note

Anna V. Q. Ross's previous poetry collections are *If a Storm* and the chapbooks *Figuring* and *Hawk Weather*. Her awards include the Robert Dana-Anhinga Prize for Poetry, the New Women's Voices Prize in Poetry, and fellowships from the Fulbright Foundation, the Massachusetts Cultural Council, Sewanee Writers' Conference, the Virginia Center for the Creative Arts, and Vermont Studio Center. Her work appears in *Harvard Review*, *The Nation*, *The Paris Review*, *The Southern Review*, and other journals. Anna is a poetry editor for *Salamander* and teaches at Tufts University, where she is a Lecturer in Poetry, and at MCI Concord through the Emerson Prison Initiative. She lives with her family in Dorchester, MA.

CPSIA information can be obtained
at www.ICGtesting.com
Printed in the USA
LVHW040023101022
730155LV00001B/2